What Our Readers Have Said...

"Although I consider myself a seasoned sales professional, it is helpful to have past learning's refreshed. The books were also beneficial because of the information concerning 'trends' in the sales relationship. The sales process should be viewed as dynamic since business relationships change regularly."

•

"For the particular business I am in and the type of sales calls I have, I find that the books in the Pinpoint Sales Training Series are very often applicable to how I conduct business. I would recommend them to other sales people, just not ones that are in my industry."

•

"These books provide very good concepts. It fits in well with the Bell Leadership training program that I attended in November."

•

"I use this material in these books and apply it to my customers and other employees I work with."

•

"I would like to know other topics. Is there anything on Production Management or Consultative Selling or Time Management?"

•

"These books are great tools that should be used as guidelines for our everyday

supervisory practices. You need to take the time to do a short self-evaluation when reading them."

•

"The Pinpoint Training Series delivers information that could be used in a lot different areas."

•

"I like this because I can take them with me to read at a convenient time. I feel the little time I have to spend in the office is best use on activities that directly relate to revenue opportunities. I like the short amount of time it takes to keep up with these."

•

"I prefer the self-study approach; it fits in with my schedule."

•

"My thought is that the real value of these books comes into effect when doing the action plans."

•

"Short and sweet. These books are easy to comprehend."

•

"I have enjoyed reading these books. They are relevant to today's work environment and the ongoing change in the way we manage our workforce."

•

"I do feel that these books have been very helpful to me at my job."

•

"I think a lot of the recommendations in these books are very useful, and can be applicable to everyday situations. If nothing else, it's a good reference guide to fall back upon if a situation arises in the future."

•

"These books are relevant to today's work environment and the ongoing change in the way we manage our workforce."

•

Dynamic Sales Communication

Pinpoint Sales Skill Development Training Series

TIMOTHY F. BEDNARZ

MAJORIUM
BUSINESS PRESS

Pinpoint Sales Skill Development Training Series
"Dynamic Sales Communication"
Timothy F. Bednarz

Graphic design: Monika Pawlak

Majorium Business Press
2025 Main Street
Stevens Point, WI 54481
715.342.1018 • 800.654.4935

ISBN 978-1-882181-81-0

Printed in the United States of America

Introduction

The Pinpoint Sales Skill Development Training Series is designed for targeted training and education regarding increased improvement in a specific skill or competency.

Each book within this series is designed to be easy to use, understand and apply to your job. It can be used as a basis for training individuals, as a discussion guide or as a personal training tool.

Each chapter within this book discusses a specific concept. When you have completed all eight chapters you should have a 360º perspective of the topic.

Additionally, each chapter is divided into specific sections:

- The first section provides you with an overview of the topic
- The Implications section discusses why the concept is important, and why it is important to learn and apply.
- The Strategies, Tips & Techniques to Apply section teaches how to use and apply the particular concept to your work.
- The Points to Ponder section gives you something to think about or to be discussed with a group setting. These are questions not meant to be immediately answered, but to be pondered over time.
- The Training Activity section provides you with the tools to transfer what you have learned to your job. It is designed to help create an action plan to effectively apply the concept.

Each of the topics in this series is time-tested and proven in the marketplace. They have been used by thousands of employees as training tools. Many of the users have commented that what made these books valuable, was the ability to refer to them when a problem surfaced. They indicated that they remembered reading about the exact problem. They referred back to these books and found an appropriate solution.

You will find them equally valuable as a resource in your professional development library.

Table of Contents

LEARNING OBJECTIVES:

- To understand the purpose of good communication.
- To effectively use communication.
- To apply effective communication techniques.
- Various communication techniques to transmit a sales message.
- To obtain results through the effective use of sales communication.

1

The Professional Communicator

The nature of the sales profession demands that salespeople be professional communicators in everything they say or do. They need to possess the skills to effectively paint a mental picture of a product's benefits and impact in the customer's or prospect's mind. They must be able to do this quickly and effectively.

IMPLICATIONS — WHAT THIS MEANS TO YOU

The salesperson of the past basically had some primary tools to communicate and sell his or her product. Most sales were made in person and supported over the telephone. Instant access via cell phones, email, fax and other communication mediums did not exist.

Today salespeople have a host of communication mediums to transmit their message instantaneously. They can research information quickly and effectively on the Internet. They are able to target and "zero in on" specific customers. They can prospect and cold call by phone, fax and email. They have the contact management and sales software to efficiently analyze a customer and tailor specific products and services to meet their needs. Salespeople have the communications power never available before.

This is important to salespeople because to sell effectively, they must learn to communicate efficiently using the best tools at their disposal. They must be able to identify the best and most effective manner to communicate their message and to move the sale forward.

This demands expertise and sophistication that most salespeople did not possess in the past.

STRATEGIES, TIPS & TECHNIQUES TO APPLY

As professional communicators, there are several simple rules that salespeople should follow if they wish to effectively convey their message in any medium. These include:

Know the Situation

Many salespeople assume they know the facts, circumstances and situations regarding the prospects they are calling on. Consequently, they develop solutions and proposals for products and services that the prospect has little or no interest in.

Before salespeople can effectively communicate their sales message, they need to gain a clear and complete view of the marketplace they are dealing in through customer, product, competitive and company knowledge. This encompasses listening to associates, non-competitive salespeople, customers and other sources of information to gain complete and comprehensive knowledge of their market and customer needs. Salespeople must take the time to read, collect and analyze information about their products and competitive offerings as well as information from trade journals, government agencies, trade associations and various other sources. They must develop knowledge and expertise before they can effectively communicate their message.

Know the Audience

During the normal course of business, salespeople will be communicating with a variety of individuals on various levels. In many organizations, salespeople must present and sell people to gain access up the line to the final decision maker(s). Not everyone is going to be concerned or interested in a full presentation, only that the salesperson is worthy of being allowed access to the next level. Therefore salespeople must know who they are talking to, what they need to know and what they are interested in. Specific sales messages must then be crafted and tailored to accomplish the objectives with that individual.

Know More than the Customer

The initial step discussed the need for the salesperson to know the situation, but they also must know what they are talking about. Prospects and customers have little time or patience to deal with the novice and uninformed salesperson. They expect the salesperson to know more than they do. It is this knowledge and expertise that gives the salesperson a "license to sell." Without it, the prospect or customer will not give them time or access. Therefore it is essential that the salesperson has knowledge and expertise about their product and service, their company, their competition, their customer and how all of this knowledge impacts the customer.

Have a Clearly Defined Objective

Salespeople must know what they want to achieve with the prospect or customer. Every call and visit must have a specific purpose and objective and be focused on moving the sale forward. Salespeople who waste the customer's time and energy will be quickly shown the door.

Represent the Company Well

Many salespeople forget that they are in front of the customer as a representative of the company that employs them. In many cases, this is the only person the customer will have contact with.

As a communicator, the salesperson must not only impart a sales message, but they must also communicate the values and image of the company because *they are the company* in the customer's eyes and will be judged as such.

POINTS TO PONDER – SOMETHING TO THINK ABOUT

1. How well do you feel you are communicating your sales message?
2. Do you communicate your message with a purpose, or is your message considered loose and unorganized?

TRAINING ACTIVITY – APPLICATION & ACTION PLAN

1. As a professional communicator, list the following five points on a sheet of paper and identify your strengths on a scale from one to five with five being the highest:
    - Know the Situation
    - Know the Audience
    - Know More than the Customer
    - Have a Clearly Defined Objective
    - Represent the Company Well
2. Based upon your personal assessment, identify what you need to do to begin communicating more effectively.

2

Six Ways Effective Communication Impacts Sales Success

The importance of communication skills and techniques and their impact on the salesperson's overall success should not be downplayed. Going beyond the simple ability to speak and carry on a conversation, in sales, effective communication means having the ability to paint a mental picture in the prospect's or customer's mind about how a specific product or service will benefit them and their business.

IMPLICATIONS — WHAT THIS MEANS TO YOU

When salespeople effectively communicate throughout the entire sales process, they experience fewer objections, stalls and barriers as well as increased customer satisfaction. This is because the customer clearly understands what they are buying and exactly what they can expect to receive. It eliminates miscommunication and misunderstandings that result in potential problems in the future.

By honing and polishing their personal communication skills, salespeople will experience increased sales, less frustration and heightened personal satisfaction.

STRATEGIES, TIPS & TECHNIQUES TO APPLY

Salespeople who deem polished and effective communication techniques unimportant should consider the impact they have on their overall success, including:

Increased Cold Calling Effectiveness

When salespeople initially contact a prospect, they typically have less than 30 seconds to communicate one or two compelling points to spark their interest. Without the use of effective communication techniques, salespeople will find it difficult to impart their message effectively and give it the power to grab a prospect's interest.

When salespeople effectively communicate their message, they will find more prospects are open to it. While it won't eliminate the rejection associated with cold calling, effective communication techniques will minimize the volume a salesperson will normally face.

More Effective Qualifying

The lack of effective qualifying techniques is the primary cause of sales barriers, objections and stalls. Qualifying is an efficient exchange of information that determines the prospect's needs, concerns, problems, interest and financial ability to make a purchase. Effective qualifying depends on good communication techniques where salespeople are versed in questioning and listening skills that allow them to probe to uncover the prospect's real needs, concerns and problems.

This goes beyond the use of open-ended questions to the use and application of specific types of inquiry that fully develop and uncover the information the salesperson needs to sell the customer or prospect.

Consistent Sales Message

Salespeople who exhibit poor communication skills often undermine their own efforts by presenting an inconsistent or mixed sales message to the prospect or customer. They fail to understand the duration of the sales process and are focused on the events of the moment. This often results in statements and messages that contradict themselves, causing confusion in the customer or prospect's mind.

Effective communication techniques compel salespeople to develop a consistent sales message that is used during the entire sales process and that is supported by their company's advertising and marketing efforts. This focuses the customer or prospect on a targeted message supported by both the salesperson and the company he or she represents.

Effectively Communicate Benefits

Prospects and customers don't buy a product, they buy what it can do for them. Unless salespeople can effectively communicate the benefits of their product or service in a clear and concise manner, they will experience delays, difficulties and frustrations. Until the prospect or customer clearly understands the benefits they are buying, they will balk at any attempts to move the sale forward.

Salespeople quite often fail to uncover the points of interest to the prospect or customer and focus on what they wish to sell, or simply make a presentation of the product's features. Such information does not communicate what the prospect or customer needs to know to make an informed buying decision.

Manage Perceptions and Expectations

Astute salespeople understand the importance of managing perceptions, as they ultimately form the expectations that the prospect or customer will have about their product or service. Sloppy or ineffective communication techniques ignore the words, statements and language that create perceptions.

Salespeople who do successfully manage the prospect's or customer's perceptions are more successful in meeting their expectations and delivering the value that sustains satisfaction.

Focused Sales Presentations

Effective communicators use the sales presentation as a tool to motivate the prospect or customer to take action. Good communication techniques inform and lead the audience to a logical conclusion that is a call to action, be it a product demonstration, trial or order.

When salespeople plan and prepare to present an effective sales presentation, they begin with the action they want the prospect or customer to take and build their presentation backward from that point. This technique allows the salesperson to lead them effectively to the point of action.

POINTS TO PONDER – SOMETHING TO THINK ABOUT

1. Have you seen how your personal communication skills may have either positively or negatively impacted your sales success?
2. Can you think of instances where the poor use of communication skills caused a major problem or resulted in a lost sale?

TRAINING ACTIVITY – APPLICATION & ACTION PLAN

1. On a sheet of paper, list the following categories:
    - Cold Calling Effectiveness
    - Qualifying
    - Consistent Sales Message
    - Effectively Communicate Benefits
    - Manage Perceptions and Expectations
    - Focused Sales Presentations
2. Evaluate your personal communication effectiveness by rating each cat-

egory using the following codes to indicate the areas that you are experiencing problems:

I. No Problems

II. Some Problems

III. Problems

IV. Many Problems

3. The areas you rated a three or higher indicate a need to examine how effectively are you communicating to a prospect or customer, including what you are doing and need to do.

3

The Causes of Communication Breakdowns

Salespeople unwittingly do specific things or demonstrate individual attitudes that hinder effective communication and repel rather than attract the customer or prospect. The ramifications include lost sales, lost customers, the inability to build and sustain long-term customer relationships, frustration and personal anxiety.

IMPLICATIONS – WHAT THIS MEANS TO YOU

There are many reasons why communication can breakdown in sales. Most of the reasons deal with personal issues of the salesperson and the emotional baggage they might bring to the job. Fortunately, once the individual salesperson can identify the causes of communication problems, they can start to work to resolve these issues and increase their overall effectiveness.

Identifying the causes of communication breakdowns is an important first step for salespeople. Most of these problems are the result of learned behaviors that with attention can be remedied. However, left unchecked, these barriers will continue to produce persistent failure and the inability of the salesperson to reach their potential.

STRATEGIES, TIPS & TECHNIQUES TO APPLY

Salespeople can be easily tripped up by a number of factors when they communicate that can affect what they say or bias them in a way that their sales message become skewed and off-focus. These factors include:

Fears

Most fears are learned and stem from past experiences or learned biases. Many stem from a deep-seated lack of self-esteem or personal confidence in one's ability to perform adequately. Many salespeople have personal fears of not meeting the customer's or prospect's expectations. They become flustered and intimidated, fearful they might say the wrong thing or make a statement that makes them appear to be ignorant of the customer's needs and concerns.

When salespeople become fearful, their ability to communicate is impaired. Rather than look foolish or be misinterpreted, they closely control their ability to effectively communicate and appear to be more sheepish than aggressive in gathering the information they need to effectively sell the customer or prospect.

Assumptions

While many assumptions made by a salesperson may be correct, communication breaks down when they accept their assumptions without fully questioning and clarifying them with the customer or prospect.

When salespeople listen to their customers and prospects, it is natural for them to make assumptions as they interpret every word, gesture, inflection and tone. However, some of those assumptions may be inaccurate and meanings may be derived that are not meant by the speaker. Communication breaks down because the salesperson thinks a specific message was conveyed when in fact the customer or prospect has said something entirely different.

Insensitivity

Communication can breakdown when there is a failure to accurately perceive the needs, feelings and concerns of others. The problem frequently occurs when salespeople ignore the customer's or prospect's stated needs and concerns and proceed to present a product or service that does not help and is of no interest to them.

Labeling

Without understanding the customer or prospect, their needs, potential size and ability to make a purchase, salespeople can often label them. Perhaps the customer's facility or personal appearance makes a poor initial impression. Automatically, the salesperson categorizes them. Once this occurs, a bias is formed that can significantly reduce the perceived opportunity the customer or prospect represents.

Uncertainty

Uncertain speaking habits arise from personal fears, mental laziness, or a conviction that one is incapable of making a valid and acceptable presentation regarding a product or service. This results in silence, stress and intimidation. Under these circumstances, the salesperson cannot either speak or listen effectively.

Resentment

Resentment is a level of personal bitterness that can destroy a salesperson's career ands personal life. Salespeople can become resentful of the customer's or prospect's position, status and income or the fact that they themselves are not working for a more prestigious company. It festers to the point that they continually look for the worst in people and situations—and often find it. This worldview taints the salesperson's perspective and colors everything that they say or do. Consequently, prospects and customers are repelled rather than attracted.

Egotism

While salespeople require a healthy ego to be successful in a profession wrought with failure and rejection, too strong of an ego conveys a lack of respect and interest in listening to a prospect or customer and identifying their needs and concerns. One of the symptoms of a strong ego is the salesperson who dominates the conversation without allowing the prospect or customer to provide input and feedback. The communication breakdown results in a failure to listen and identify the true needs of the customer, which leads to poor sales, numerous objections, stalls, barriers and poor customer retention.

POINTS TO PONDER — SOMETHING TO THINK ABOUT

1. Have you experienced problems and barriers to your success that could be attributed to the causes of communication breakdowns listed above?
2. Do you have a sense that something has been holding you back, yet you are unable to pinpoint exactly what?

TRAINING ACTIVITY — APPLICATION & ACTION PLAN

1. Perform a self-evaluation of your communication skills and identify any causes of breakdowns.
2. Review the following list of causes and determine whether any of them apply to you.
3. Once you are aware of what problems may be occurring, assess what you think causes them and what actions you need to take to rectify them.
    - Fears
    - Assumptions
    - Insensitivity
    - Labeling
    - Uncertainty
    - Resentment
    - Egotism

4

Developing Positive Communication's Traits

When thinking of communicating effectively, the first thought is that one must be eloquent and intelligent. Individuals who have this perception are focusing on how something is being communicated rather than on what is being communicated. It is the old argument of form over substance. However, it is the personality of the salesperson that actually counts and their personal attitude that helps or hinders communication.

IMPLICATIONS – WHAT THIS MEANS TO YOU

The success of sales communication depends to a large extent on the personality traits of the salesperson. As previously discussed, many communication breakdowns are caused by personal problems, attitudes and conflicts that a salesperson brings to his or her job. Once salespeople understand what may be causing communication breakdowns and failures, they can take the necessary steps to modify or alter it. However, there are positive personality traits that can facilitate effective communication.

This is important for salespeople because when they understand the traits that can both help or hinder their communication, they can learn to effectively manage them. Most individuals go through life without ever understanding how these traits can transform their lives in either direction.

STRATEGIES, TIPS & TECHNIQUES TO APPLY

Since effective communication is a personal issue, it stands to reason that there are positive communication traits a salesperson can develop, including:

Self-Awareness

Self-awareness is a personal understanding on one's attitudes and convictions, how they were formed and how they can be adapted and modified to maximize one's performance. It helps the salesperson to understand his or her values and beliefs and that these are worth sharing with others.

Some salespeople may not consider self-awareness to be an important trait or one that has any application to them. However, it is a salesperson's core beliefs, attitude and convictions that motivates him or her and shapes how they will sell a product or service or treat a customer.

Understanding

Before salespeople can effectively sell their product or service, they must have the personal desire to fully understand a customer's needs, concerns and problems. While this may seem elementary on the surface, the truth is many salespeople simply do not have this desire. They have a desire to sell a product or service, pocket the commission, and move on to the next prospect with little or no concern for the customer and the consequences of the purchase. This is precisely the customer's fear: the salesperson will quickly disappear after the sale.

Successful salespeople have the desire to understand their customers. They communicate this desire with the use of effective questioning techniques to probe for hidden needs and concerns. Additionally, they question all of their assumptions and clarify the customer's statements and expectations to avoid any miscommunication.

Care and Concern

When salespeople focus on their personal need to get the sale, their motivation is transparent. The customer knows that they are not concerned with their needs and problems and therefore quickly stops listening.

Salespeople may wonder how a customer can sense this. It is because with their words, actions, gestures and facial expressions this message is clearly communicated even when a salesperson attempts to mask it. Individuals can sense genuine concern and empathy for their needs and concerns. When salespeople are warm, interested and caring, they automatically open the doors to effective communication.

Emotional Control

Salespeople have the ability to control their personal emotions once they understand that negative emotions such as anger, bitterness and hostility produce no positive effects and actually prevent them from achieving their goals.

Salespeople can become victims of anger, frustration, depression, envy, resentment and jealousy, or they can have the fortitude to rise above them. Negative emotions do not have a place in a salesperson's life and only serve to hinder their growth, productivity, effectiveness and personal happiness. Fully understanding this, any salesperson boxed in by their emotions can motivate themselves to change.

Self-Esteem

Healthy self-esteem is a key element for every salesperson. It is the personal strength that allows each to overcome the continuous failure and rejection associated with the sales profession.

Low self-esteem is the consequence of a salesperson accepting someone else's standard of his or her self-worth. Often these individuals judge others on the superficial values of beauty, money or popularity.

Each individual is unique and endowed with his or her own skills and talents. Developing healthy self-esteem depends on recognizing these skills and accepting them while avoiding attempts to meet another person's expectations.

Self-Confidence

A salesperson's self-confidence is based upon his or her self-esteem and means they can trust and rely on their personal resources and judgment in any situation. This allows salespeople to take the necessary risks to be successful while meeting new situations and confidently selling their product or service to prospects and strangers without fear, even knowing that some will turn them down or not buy from them. They have the confidence to learn from their mistakes and not take them to heart.

Sharing

When salespeople sell customers and build relationships with them, they must give and share of themselves. This means sharing a personal commitment for the customer's success as well as their expertise and experience to ensure their satisfaction.

Successful selling today means salespeople must be able to give generously of themselves to build and sustain a customer relationship. It means focusing on the customer rather than on their personal wants and needs, knowing full well that if the customer is satisfied, their needs will also be met.

POINTS TO PONDER — SOMETHING TO THINK ABOUT

1. Are you aware of the positive and negative communication patterns and traits that you exhibit?
2. Are there positive traits that you were not aware were associated with effective communication?

TRAINING ACTIVITY — APPLICATION & ACTION PLAN

Salespeople often express negative communication patterns without being aware of it.

1. For the next week, record your conversations by either writing them down or tape recording them.
2. Take notes and analyze your communication habits for negative habits and patterns.

5

Creating an Effective Sales Letter

Many customers and prospects have built an impregnable electronic wall around themselves. In many cases, it is impossible to make contact with these buyers since they refuse to respond to voice and email. In these instances, a sales letter sent by regular mail or fax could be an effective method of penetrating the "electronic veil" and gaining their attention.

IMPLICATIONS – WHAT THIS MEANS TO YOU

Sales letters are not impersonal direct mail pieces. These are letters that are specifically addressed to a decision maker that demonstrates the salesperson's knowledge of their business and the actions that he or she can take to assist the prospect to solve a problem, meet a need or improve their business. Each letter is written with the exact needs of the individual prospect in mind.

There is a great deal of reliance on new methods of communication to contact prospects and build customers. However, there are times when a well-written letter to the decision maker might be the best means of opening the door. The key is to craft it in a personal and applicable way that demonstrates a personal knowledge of the prospect's business concerns, needs and problems.

STRATEGIES, TIPS & TECHNIQUES TO APPLY

Effective sales letters are similar to cold calls. They must move quickly to grab the prospect's attention and spark his or her interest. If they fail to do so they will be quickly relegated to the wastebasket.

The following techniques will strengthen sales letters and help ensure that they get read.

Attention Getter

The first paragraph of the sales letter must grab the reader's attention. The best way salespeople can do this is to state their strongest benefit in the first sentence. One effective technique is to phrase the benefit in the form of a question such as, " If you could (state the benefit) would you be interested?" The stronger the benefit, the more likely it is to spark the reader's interest and keep them reading.

Establish a Bond

The second step for the salesperson to follow is to establish a bond of mutual self-interest with the reader that demonstrates how he or she can assist them. An effective technique for salespeople to use is a short case study or testimonial that clearly demonstrates the salesperson's ability to help his or her customers solve their problems and build their business.

Communicate Benefits

Once salespeople have demonstrated with a story or testimonial that they can help the customer, they should state how they can be of further service to them by clearly outlining the benefits that he or she is capable of delivering to their business. It should be noted that an effective sales letter communicates benefits, not features. The letter must clearly communicate what the salesperson can do for the reader's business, and a list of product features will not accomplish that.

Refer

The letter should refer the reader to an enclosed brochure, reply card or website that provides him or her with additional information in more detail. If the salesperson leaves out this critical step, he or she will reduce the impact of the letter.

Ask for Action

The final step is to ask the reader to take immediate action. Depending on the product the salesperson is selling, this might include an order, product trial or sales inquiry. In the age of cyberspace, refer the reader to a phone number, website or email address that allows them to take immediate action. Otherwise it is too easy to put the letter aside for future action, even if they are interested in the offer.

Length

Many salespeople will write one-page sales letters because they feel the prospect will not read a longer letter. Statistics indicate that a long letter will "outpull" a short letter in every type of business. A sales letter of three to four pages would not be considered too long provided it is well constructed, effectively communicates the sales message and does not ramble.

The idea is to state a problem and a solution. Many individuals feel that a problem that can be solved with a single page solution isn't worth their time and money.

POINTS TO PONDER — SOMETHING TO THINK ABOUT

1. How often do you use sales letters to communicate your sales message to a prospect?
2. Do you individually draft a sales letter, or do you use a canned presentation for your format?

TRAINING ACTIVITY — APPLICATION & ACTION PLAN

1. Select a prospect that you have not been able to reach.
2. Create a sales letter that seizes their interest by stating an immediate benefit, establishes a bond through the use of a sales story or testimonial, communicates the benefits your product or service can provide, refers them to a promotional piece or website for more detail and asks for action.
3. Draft and proof this letter and mail or fax to the prospect.

6

Sales Presentations Must Be Designed Around the Close

If salespeople wish to convey their sales message effectively, they must take the time and care to prepare what they wish to communicate, draw the prospect or customer to a logical conclusion, and lead him or her to action.

Not every sales call or presentation will result in a sale, but it should result in some form of action that moves the prospect one step forward toward the sale. This cannot be done haphazardly, but must be accomplished in a planned and premeditated fashion.

IMPLICATIONS – WHAT THIS MEANS TO YOU

Many salespeople tend to "wing it" during their sales calls. Even if they have an objective stated for a specific call, once in front of the customer or prospect, there is an inclination to see what develops and to react accordingly. Consequently, the call objectives are either left unmet or only marginally fulfilled.

With the high costs associated with making a physical sales call, every minute of face time with the prospect or customer must count. It is important for salespeople to appreciate that most sales are either won or lost before the sales call is ever made. Sales are won with thorough and painstaking preparation.

Many salespeople don't believe in this concept, trusting their instincts and acting accordingly. But the time invested in preparation can dramatically reduce the time it takes to close the sale.

STRATEGIES, TIPS & TECHNIQUES TO APPLY

Salespeople must understand that the most important part of a presentation is the close. It is where they either accomplish their objective or fail. Most salespeople probably understand this concept, but fail to realize that they have only one opportunity to make a professional close. This is where adequate preparation comes into play.

When salespeople adequately prepare their presentations, they are able to build them from the close backward. In this manner, everything they say or do at the beginning and during the body of the presentation focuses the prospect or customer on the close. This is not unlike a trial lawyer's closing statement: it leads off with a strong component and, as they will remember what they hear last, closes with the element that makes the biggest impact on the prospect or customer.

No salesperson can hope to communicate well and effectively move a prospect or customer forward by reacting. Adequate preparation allows the salesperson to build their argument and move the prospect or customer to the objective or close. This is not possible unless time is invested to develop a powerful presentation.

A well-designed presentation should start with an opening that conceptually conveys the criteria or functions of the product or service.

The body of the presentation presents the functions, features, benefits and advantages.

The close summarizes the strengths and demonstrates that they are the same as the characteristics, criteria and functions of the ideal solution.

Each step of the sales presentation supports the others and focuses the prospect on the ideal solution to their problem or concern. They are lead through a logical thought process that reinforces itself every step of the way. The close provides the answers to the questions raised during the opening. If the prospect or customer agrees with the opening and the body of the presentation, the close brings him or her to the action point.

None of this occurs through happenstance. Salespeople who wish to lead their customers and prospects to this point must take the time to prepare and design their presentation from the close backward. The entire presentation is only as good as the close. Salespeople only have one chance to do it right and make it memorable. This takes planning and cannot be accomplished by winging it.

POINTS TO PONDER — SOMETHING TO THINK ABOUT

1. How much time and preparation do you devote to your sales calls and presentations?
2. Compare the results of planned sales calls and presentations to those where you have winged it.

TRAINING ACTIVITY — APPLICATION & ACTION PLAN

1. Design a sales presentation from the close backwards:
2. Determine the actions you wish the prospect or customer to take.
3. Identify the strongest impact statement you can make to motivate the prospect or customer.
4. Create a strong closing statement.
5. Build your opening statement by presenting the characteristics and criteria that you will communicate in your close.
6. Develop the functions, features, benefits and advantages that focus the prospect or customer on the close.
7. Develop a strong closing statement and commit it to memory.

7

Negative Communication Styles Tarnish Your Image

Sales communication is based upon accurately applying the right techniques for transferring a salesperson's thoughts and messages directly to the customer during the various phases of the selling process. Effectively using the most successful methods for communicating their sales message creates their "image." Negative communication styles tarnish a salesperson's professional communication and sales image.

IMPLICATIONS – WHAT THIS MEANS TO YOU

All salespeople possess the ability to speak fluently and communicate relatively well. Yet there are times when they can easily stumble during a discussion with the customer, especially when a particular issue or circumstance catches them off-guard. When this occurs salespeople often resort to using one of three negative communication styles.

When salespeople find themselves in a stressful situation, they tend to assume a defensive and negative communication style. Often this is done unconsciously, but the results can nevertheless be detrimental to the sale. This is because the customer observes, weighs and judges their overall performance as impacted by the salesperson's professional communication image.

STRATEGIES, TIPS & TECHNIQUES TO APPLY

Salespeople must maintain an effective communication image and style as an effective tool to meet the customer's needs and solve their problems and concerns. More importantly, effective communication must move the customer or prospect continually forward toward a commitment. Negative communication styles interfere with this process.

There are three basic negative communication styles that may mirror a salesperson's personal traits. Addressing each improves overall communications with customers and prospects.

The 'I'm Sorry' Style

In the "I'm sorry" style, the salesperson is continually apologizing for his or her words and actions. It is often seen in salespeople who have a need to seek approval from other individuals. At its most extreme, this style is excessively focused on the customer to the detriment of the sales message. When a salesperson offers numerous apologies, overdone explanations and repeated phrases and sentences, it negatively affects the clarity and professional image of the message.

Rather than giving themselves time to think during pauses, salespeople will use fillers and get carried away on a tangent that causes them to lose focus and direction. Consequently, customers begin to question their credibility.

There is a positive side to this style, as salespeople generally only exhibit a few of these characteristics rather than all of them. Most of the time salespeople who fall into this style compensate with excellent nonverbal communication, using smiles, displaying friendly eyes and positive nods. The most undesirable habits are easily diminished with confidence and assertiveness building.

The 'Commanding' Style

In the commanding style of communication, the salesperson dominates the conversation. Salespeople who use this style generally display perfect control over the conversation. They are polished communicators—except they have a tendency to focus on themselves, not the customer. Their words and phrases display high levels of energy, yet at the same time suggest to the customer they have "earned the right" to impart their knowledge and opinions.

Depending upon their own style of communicating, customers can react positively or negatively to this approach. Salespeople using the commanding style often lack the patience to listen for details and reasons. Their phrases, tone and inflections often convey an attitude suggesting little concern for what the customer thinks. Consequently, the sales message often leaves the customer less than impressed with the salesperson and what he or she has to say. The result is a lost customer.

The positive side of the commanding style is in the salesperson's ability to be articulate, well-organized and creative. They are effectively able to use their memory to impart facts and details in a concerned manner with open-ended questions. This brings the customer's perspective into the open regarding problems, situations and solutions.

Salespeople who habitually fall into the commanding style often forget it is easier to analyze situations when they take the time to slow down and improve their active listening skills.

The 'Machine' Style

The machine style is used when salespeople communicate too much and listen too little. Salespeople who fall into this style of communicating generally exhibit strength in problem solving and recognizing solutions because of a tendency to be factual. Additionally, these salespeople are adept at effectively using silences. They find this style comfortable because it provides a functional wall with which to fend off emotional threats.

This mode of communication can easily create negative interference within the selling process. Some customers interpret the salesperson's longer pauses and silences as a sign of hostility.

When using this style, salespeople are unaware of thinking and talking speeds for better customer understanding and can instead create tension. A lack of regard for the customer's time produces impatience on their part to get to the heart of the sales message.

Sales messages from the "machine communicator" are strong in content and ideas but emotionally weak. To overcome a depersonalized sales message, it is important to develop insights that convey greater in-depth understanding of the customer's needs and concerns.

The best way salespeople can overcome the machine style is to be more aware of how they evaluate a situation and assess the information heard while engaged in the sales process, not after all the input has been gathered and discussed. A salesperson can turn this negative style into a positive approach when they are able to help customers who are struggling to prioritize issues, concerns and problems. This is helpful when these issues and concerns are more complex or when multiple factors need to be addressed to solve their problems.

POINTS TO PONDER – SOMETHING TO THINK ABOUT

1. What is your natural reaction or tendency when placed in a stressful situation by a customer?
2. Can you think of any specific situations when these personal tendencies harmed the sales process or resulted in a lost sale?

TRAINING ACTIVITY – APPLICATION & ACTION PLAN

1. Perform a self-analysis of your communication style. On a sheet of paper list the three styles:
   - I'm Sorry
   - Commanding
   - Machine
2. Ask yourself the following questions that apply to each and rate your responses on a scale of 1 to 10 with ten being the worst in personal tendencies.

- Do I often apologize for my words or actions?
- Do I tend to dominate the conversation with my customers?
- Do I tend to present too much and listen too little?

The higher the score in each category, the stronger the tendency to use a specific style and the need to address and modify your communication approach.

8

Interpreting Body Language

It has been claimed that as much as 90% of all communication is nonverbal. To communicate effectively, salespeople must be skilled in understanding and interpreting what is being communicated to them. All too often salespeople fail to notice the nonverbal cues displaying clear signs of either interest or disinterest in what they are presenting.

IMPLICATIONS — WHAT THIS MEANS TO YOU

The concept of understanding body language has been around for decades and was popularized by several books on the topic published in the early 1970s. Highly effective salespeople understand the need to be master communicators and this includes mastery of nonverbal communication. Once these skills are acquired, most individuals become intensely aware of nonverbal cues, and understanding the totality of what is being communicated to them comes as easily as talking and listening.

It is important for people to master the skill of interpreting body language as it provides subtle but valuable feedback while speaking with an associate or coworker. Accurate interpretations allow them to quickly adapt their remarks as they speak in response to the reactions of the other person. Salespeople who ignore nonverbal cues and pay attention only to the words spoken place themselves at a distinct disadvantage.

STRATEGIES, TIPS & TECHNIQUES TO APPLY

There are some general and subtle gestures that salespeople should be aware of that can assist them in their sales efforts. These include:

Eyes

The eyes are an important area to observe in any conversation. Honest people have a tendency to look the person they are speaking to straight in the eyes. Dishonest people or individuals with something to hide will tend to allow their eyes to dart and shift throughout a conversation. However, there may be other interpretations. Shy or subservient personalities will tend to look downward during a conversation. Additionally, an individual may glance away or appear distracted if they are either uninterested or uncomfortable with the conversation.

When an uncomfortable question is asked, most individuals will avoid eye contact. Individuals should be aware of this. The primary focus should be on a desire to build trust and reduce tension rather than putting the individual on the spot and increasing discomfort.

Salespeople should be attuned to several eye gestures. If the other person looks upward with a fixed expression or blinks rapidly, it is highly likely that what is being discussed is being seriously considered. If the listener raises one eyebrow, they are displaying disbelief, while raising two eyebrows shows surprise or possible complete disbelief.

Face

Some individuals have very demonstrative and easy-to-read faces. They readily elicit emotional responses with smiles, frowns, nods of the head and other nonverbal cues that can be easily interpreted. However, many people in business have learned to assume a poker face that is very difficult to interpret. Some customers will be extremely guarded and keep all emotional gestures and cues in check in order to not prematurely betray their positions.

Hands

What individuals do with their hands around their face reveals a great deal about their attitudes and emotions. Casually rubbing the eye with one finger can mean the listener is unsure about what is being said. Placing the head in an open palm and dropping the chin in a nodding manner while allowing eyelids to droop communicates boredom. Placing a hand to the cheek or stroking the chin generally shows interest or consideration or a concentrated focus on what to say as a response.

Additionally, drumming of the fingers demonstrates impatience, a lack of interest or a clouding of the mind with pressing issues other than the sales topic being presented. Fidgeting can indicate that the listener is uncomfortable with the conversation or is hiding information or other necessary input.

Arms and Legs

Tightly crossed arms may indicate the listener is in a defensive posture. Individuals who cross their legs may be disagreeing with what is being said. Crossed arms and legs generally display an extremely negative attitude toward what is being communicated. Individuals should be careful in their interpretations. Sometimes arms are crossed because the room is cool and the other person is simply cold or uncomfortable.

Open and outstretched arms are most often a sign the other person is open to what is being said or that he or she is in full agreement.

Combined Meanings

It is important for individuals to remember that all of the obvious signs—the eyes, face, arms, legs and hands—are working in unison with each other. With a little care, individuals should readily be able to interpret the entire body posture as open, threatening, uninterested, honest, resistant, etc. They should be able to match the words with the posture and efficiently read between the lines.

POINTS TO PONDER — SOMETHING TO THINK ABOUT

1. How conscious are you of the body language and posture of the individuals you encounter?
2. Do you make a conscious effort to not only hear what the person you are speaking to is saying with their words, but also what they are conveying with their body language?

TRAINING ACTIVITY — APPLICATION & ACTION PLAN

1. Over the next week, make a conscious effort to observe the body language of every individual you come in contact with.
2. As you interpret the body language, question the individual about their posture.
    - If their arms are crossed, ask them if they disagree with you.
    - If their arms are open, ask if they agree with you.
3. Use this method to confirm your interpretations.

About the Author

Timothy F. Bednarz, Ph.D. is CEO of the American Management Development Group, Inc. For over 20 years he has researched, designed and authored hundreds of learning and development programs used by Fortune 1000 companies.

He is also the author of *Great! What Makes Leaders Great. What They Did, How They Did It and What You Can Learn from It* (2011).

Speaking Availability

Timothy F. Bednarz, Ph.D. is available for speaking engagements for your next meeting or association event. He can be contacted at 800-654-4935 or by e-mail at timothy.bednarz@majorium.com.

Bulk Sales

Bulk sales of this book or any other titles available from Majorium Business Press. Inquiries can be directed to sales@majorium.com, or by phone at 800-6654-4935.

Quick Order Form

Fax orders: 715-342-1118. Send this form.

Telephone orders: Call 800-654-4935 toll-free. Have your credit card ready.

Email orders: sales@majorium.com

Postal orders: Majorium Business Press, 2025 Main Street, Stevens Point, WI 54481, USA.

Please send the following books:

____

____

____

____

Please send more FREE information on:

❑Catalog ❑Speaking/Seminars ❑Mailing Lists ❑Consulting

Name: ____

Address: ____

City: ______________________ State: _____ Zip: _________

Telephone: ______________________________________

Email address: ___________________________________

Sales tax: Please add 5.5% for products shipped to Wisconsin addresses.

Shipping by air:

United States: $4.00 for first book and $2.00 for each additional product.

International: $9.00 for first book; $5.00 for each additional product (estimate).

Made in the USA
Monee, IL
08 November 2026

67382867R00031